"Losing a child is a peculiar grief. All griefs have their own way of breaking our souls, but to lose a child that you never met stays with you your whole life. But like all things Christian, when we do them by faith, a peculiar resurrection is born in our hearts, because Jesus is at work in all our deaths. The apostle Paul calls it a 'fellowship of his suffering.' Let Jackie guide you into that fellowship. This book is for everyone, not just those of us who've lost a child, because we all need to let our customized suffering draw us into Christ."

Paul Miller, Author of *J-curve*, *A Praying Life*, and *A Praying Church*

"*You Are Still a Mother* is not only a book for mothers suffering the loss of an infant; it is a book for all Christians, both men and women. I am now eighty years old, and Jackie's practical wisdom (learned through suffering) has deepened my understanding of the ways of God and has provided me with daily solace. This is a book to be read, reread, dog-eared, and read again!"

Barbara Hughes, Author of *Disciplines of a Godly Woman*

"Deeply personal and richly biblical, Jackie Gibson's book guides bereaved mothers to the Father of mercies. This is not a book about getting past grief, however. It is about walking with God by faith, even while empty arms ache for a missing child, and living in hope of glory."

Joel Beeke, President, Puritan Reformed Theological Seminary, Grand Rapids, MI

"This lovely book is proof that things beautiful can grow from sorrows unspeakable. Jackie Gibson has found a way of lending her story of loss to others lost in darkness and overcome with grief in a way that shines light on the path ahead. In communion with others who have suffered in similar ways, with raw honesty but gentleness, she charts a journey of learning not to ~~...~~ stand but to trust the One your side. These pages wil unique heartache, and the love of God in a profoundl

David Gibson, Minist of *The Lord of Psalm 2:*

"This beautiful book captures both the profound devastation of losing a child through stillbirth or miscarriage, as well as the profound hope in God that is available in the midst of loss. It is a terrible thing to go through a pregnancy with all its anticipation and then to have empty arms. This book provides caring companionship and hope for healing for those who face this complicated grief."

Nancy Guthrie, Author of *Hearing Jesus Speak into Your Sorrow*

"This is the story of Jackie Gibson and of Leila, her beloved stillborn daughter. It is heartrendingly honest but also profound. And the hands that composed these sentences while drenched in tears also carry keys that open doors of hope. While written especially for Jackie Gibson's sisters in sorrow, *You Are Still a Mother* is a gift to the whole church."

Sinclair Ferguson, Preaching Associate, Trinity Church, Aberdeen; author of *The Whole Christ*

"In *You Are Still a Mother*, Jackie Gibson gently connects the grieving heart of a mother-to-be and the sympathizing heart of the Lord Jesus Christ. This beautiful little book ministered to my wife and me and we will be using it to minister to others. Thank you, Jackie."

Dane Ortlund, Senior Pastor, Naperville Presbyterian Church; author of *Gentle and Lowly*

"The pain a mother experiences is like none other. It is the personal pain of loss, the pain for the little one you loved before meeting them, and the loss of a relationship before you've ever had the chance to enjoy it. Jackie has taken her heartbreak and has used it to bring words of consolation and life to those in need. Be deeply comforted by her reminder that the Lord is good, even in the midst of suffering. He will sustain you."

Julie Lowe, Christian Counselor, CCEF; author of *Safeguards*

YOU ARE STILL A MOTHER

HOPE FOR WOMEN GRIEVING A STILLBIRTH OR MISCARRIAGE

Jackie Gibson

newgrowthpress.com

New Growth Press, Greensboro, NC 27401
newgrowthpress.com
Copyright © 2023 by Jackie Gibson

Cover Design: Faceout Books, faceoutstudio.com
Interior Typesetting & eBook: Lisa Parnell, lparnellbookservices.com

ISBN 978-1-64507-341-3 (Print)
ISBN 978-1-64507-342-0 (eBook)

Library of Congress Cataloging-in-Publication Data
Names: Gibson, Jackie, 1985– author.
Title: You are still a mother : hope for women grieving a stillbirth or
    miscarriage / Jackie Gibson.
Description: Greensboro, NC : New Growth Press, [2023] | Includes
    bibliographical references. | Summary: "A companion through the
    emotions, questions, and feelings that arise when grieving a stillbirth
    or miscarriage, providing reassurance that God offers comfort"—
    Provided by publisher.
Identifiers: LCCN 2023017825 (print) | LCCN 2023017826 (ebook) | ISBN
    9781645073413 (Print) | ISBN 9781645073420 (e-book)
Subjects: LCSH: Children—Death—Religious aspects—Christianity. |
    Stillbirth—Religious aspects—Christianity. | Miscarriage—Religious
    aspects—Christianity. | Grief—Religious aspects—Christianity. |
    Hope—Religious aspects—Christianity. | Consolation.
Classification: LCC BV4907 .G49 2023 (print) | LCC BV4907 (ebook) |
    DDC 248.8/66—dc23/eng/20230602
LC record available at https://lccn.loc.gov/2023017825
LC ebook record available at https://lccn.loc.gov/2023017826

Printed in the United States of America

30 29 28 27 26 25 24 23   1 2 3 4 5

For Sarah

Who knows the weight of Leila in her arms, and can remember with me that she was, indeed, beautiful.

In Memoriam

Esther

John

Hugo

Leila

James

Freddy

Hannah

Joseph

Robert

Aria

They died at the commandment of the Lord. They would have willingly stayed; but they gladly went.

John Brown

Contents

Acknowledgments	viii
Preface	xi
1. Leila	1
2. The Everlasting Arms	8
3. Man of Sorrows	14
4. Written in His Book	21
5. Things Too Wonderful for Me	26
6. Precious in His Sight	33
7. You Are Still a Mother	41
8. Safe in His Arms	47
9. The Pain Will Change	53
10. All Things for Good?	59
11. Heaven Is Our Home	65
12. After Winter, Spring	71
Last Words: A Prayer to Join Our Children	78
Suggestions for Further Reading	79
Endnotes	81

Acknowledgments

Working on a project like this is humbling for many reasons, one of them being the realization that you cannot do it alone. I am so grateful for all the people the Lord provided to enable me to bring this book to completion.

Barbara Juliani from New Growth Press (NGP) had a heart for the book from the very beginning, and I am thankful for her encouragement and prayers. She edited the manuscript as both a skilled writer, and perhaps more importantly, as a mother who has experienced deep loss. Her thoughtful sensitivity has enhanced each page. Ruth Castle, NGP's editorial project manager, helped to keep this project on track. And Dan Stelzer, who oversaw the cover, came up with such a hope-filled design. I am appreciative of Sarah Phillips, who graciously carved out time in her busy life to provide excellent editorial feedback. Thanks also to Desiring God for their permission to use excerpts from a blog post that originally appeared on their website: desiringgod.org. Capitol CMG Licensing also kindly granted permission to quote the hymn "See What a Morning," by Stuart Townend and Keith Getty.

While I rejoice in the sound of small feet pattering around my house, it makes finding time to write difficult. So I am grateful to Bethany Kueh for freeing me up by looking after Zac and Hannah many mornings, and to Lydia for being the sweetest playmate.

There is no way this book would have been completed without the unceasing encouragement and help from my husband, Jonny. He was endlessly generous with his time, always willing to pause his own work to talk through chapters and help me find clarity in my thoughts and words. One of the reasons he loves this project so much is because he is a father who loves to talk about his daughter Leila. He is so proud to be her dad. I treasure the times we remember her together and appreciate how he doesn't hold back the tears of his fatherly affection. I can't wait to see him hug his daughter again one day.

In my darkest days of loss, God set aside one particular friend for a special purpose, a friend who became family while our own was far away—Sarah Dixon, to whom I dedicate this book. I may not have known it back on that famous Guy Fawkes Night, but God knew that I needed a friend like her—a friend for seasons of joy and laughter, and a friend for a season of sorrow. She stepped right into the dark places with us, caring for Ben at such a confusing time for him, bringing him to the hospital, and being one of the very few people who held our little girl. It means so much to have a friend with an actual memory of my daughter, who is never shy to talk about her. She will forever be one of my dearest friends.

This book is written in memoriam of a list of very precious babies whose lives, though short, have spoken the hope of the gospel to me in beautiful ways. Their mothers are all women who love the Lord Jesus, the Man of Sorrows, and who resemble him with the scars they have received through suffering. Whenever I think of their families, I remember the baby missing from their homes, the baby who now lives in heaven. These women don't get to hear the name of their son or daughter spoken often, so it is an honor to write their names here. It warms my heart to think of these little lambs enfolded in the arms of their Good Shepherd, on another shore, in a greater light. One day soon, we will join them.

Preface

This is a club no one wants to be in. If you are reading this book, it is likely you are part of the sad solidarity of mothers who carry around the hidden grief of a baby who died. C. S. Lewis described the beginning of friendship as the moment two companions meet and discover: "'What? You too? I thought I was the only one.' . . . And instantly they stand together in an immense solitude."[1] Stillbirth or miscarriage is not something we want to have in common, and I wish you didn't have a reason to pick up this book. But while you stand in the solitude of your grief, there are mothers all over the world who stand there too. I am one of them. Even though your arms are empty, I know your heart carries your baby with you wherever you go. Though in this instance you have nothing to show for your motherhood, you are still a mother. You will always be the mother of your child who died.

This book is the story of the death of my daughter Leila. I'm sure as you read there will be parts that feel familiar, details that you recognize in your story, the

"What? You too?" moments. There will also be parts that are different from yours. As I have heard my husband say many times, "Each person's valley is each person's valley." But there is one character who is the same in all our stories. It is the God who made our precious children, and who called them home. This story is about him, and how he is always good, even in the darkness.

My prayer is that as you read this book, you will see that the God who was faithful in my story will be faithful in yours too.

> For the LORD is good;
>   his steadfast love endures forever,
>   and his faithfulness to all generations.
>
> (Psalm 100:5)

1

Leila

I loved thee, daughter of my heart;
My child, I loved thee dearly;
And though we only met to part,
How sweetly! How severely!
Nor life nor death can sever
My soul from thine forever.

"A Mother's Lament"
James Montgomery

FROM WOMB TO TOMB

This is the story of our dark-haired baby girl who died when the daffodils were blooming.

It was Sunday night, March 13, 2016, and I was a week away from my due date. I phoned the hospital from our home in Cambridge, England, concerned about my baby's reduced movement. I was encouraged by a nurse to stay home, drink something cold, and count kicks. I did feel movements that day, gentle though they were; my husband Jonny felt them too, his hand stretched across my full-term pregnant belly. When I phoned the nurse again and told her the number of kicks we had felt, she reassured me that there was no reason to come in. Little did we know, they were good-bye kicks, of a kind.

The next morning I woke up feeling uneasy, unsure if I had felt any movement from my baby. Jonny and I drove to the hospital, trying to make light conversation, but deep down we knew something was wrong. In the examination room, a cheerful nurse got out a fetal Doppler to listen for a heartbeat: "Now let's see where this baby is hiding!" As the wand traveled all over my stomach, her chipper demeanor quickly faded. My heartbeat could be heard, but not the familiar galloping heartbeat of a baby. She tried another Doppler, but still no heartbeat could be found. She went to get the ultrasound machine to check more thoroughly, and as she left, she pulled the curtain around our cubicle. I gripped Jonny's hand, holding my breath, willing all of this not to be true.

The nurse returned, followed by new medical staff, who gathered around us like ominous, storm clouds. "There's no heartbeat, is there?" I asked urgently, but they refused to answer until they were certain. The ultrasound machine was wheeled in, and just as they were about to put the wand on my belly, the machine shut down and stopped working. More waiting. Another machine was located, but it too had technical difficulties and refused to start. After an agonizing fifteen minutes, it was finally working. I couldn't look at the screen, so afraid of what I might see. Instead I stared at my husband's face, who watched our baby's body appear on the grainy monitor. The tears were already streaming when, finally, the words we didn't want to hear cut through the silence:

"I'm sorry. There is no heartbeat."

My heart cracked open and a terrible grief spread through my whole body. I didn't make a sound, but the tears increased and I started to shake. Jonny wept loudly, crying out, "No! No! No! It cannot be!" But it was. I asked if it was a boy or a girl as we had waited for it to be a surprise. I still couldn't look at the screen— "I think it's a girl." A girl! God had given us a daughter. And taken her away.

After the pronouncement of death, I asked the doctors to wheel me straight into surgery for a Cesarean section. Surely they would take the baby out right away! But they gently explained that I would have to give birth naturally. What!? How could they expect me to go through labor when I was already in unbearable agony? I wanted to be under anesthetic immediately, so I could sleep through the horror of what was unfolding. No alternate path was offered. We had no choice but to go home and wait for labor to begin.

On the outside, I looked indistinguishable from any other pregnant woman nearing her due date. That same afternoon, we took our four-year-old to a playground. We were in complete shock but our new reality didn't erase our son's need for some semblance of normalcy (and we didn't have family living close by). I bumped into an acquaintance who excitedly asked when I was due. I couldn't bear to explain, so I just gave her my due date and left it at that. Little did she know that my womb had become a tomb.

The days between our daughter dying and waiting to give birth were the darkest of my life. The only thing that brought us relief was sleep, fitful though it was, punctuated by graphic nightmares. There was a moment after waking when I'd desperately hope it had all been a strange dream, but then I would look at my round stomach and feel the stillness. No kicks. No hiccups. No life. And then the crushing remembrance of what had happened would come flooding back. I was so afraid of giving birth to a dead baby. The terror of what was ahead overwhelmed me, and I spent most of those days lying in bed in stunned silence, weeping and listening to a few songs on repeat.

WE ONLY MET TO PART

Three days later, we drove to the hospital in the early hours of a misty morning, labor finally underway. Miraculously, the Lord gave us peace which surpassed all understanding, and we were ready to meet our daughter. We were ushered to a special room in the labor and delivery suite set apart for sad circumstances like ours. As we walked toward it, we passed the room where our son had been born four years earlier. Death and life only doors apart.

Labor was intense, but mercifully short—thirty-seven minutes in total! Our baby was born at 10:25 a.m. inside a fully intact amniotic sac. With no living baby bearing down, my waters never broke. Usually, the groans of labor culminate in the wondrous sound of a crying baby. But this delivery suite was filled with deathly silence as we beheld our beautiful, still daughter—a sister to Ben, a niece, a cousin, a granddaughter, a great-granddaughter. She weighed seven pounds, her head was covered with dark hair, and she had a nose like her big brother's. Her balled-up fist was resting under her chin, as if she was deep in thought. We named her Leila Judith Grace. Leila (pronounced "Lay-la"), simply because we love the name; Judith, after her great-grandmother from Sydney, Australia; and Grace, because God graced us with a long-awaited second child.

Death had already marred her body. Limp and floppy, she had no muscle tone, and her pale skin had started to peel. But despite these signs of death, we could still see so much beauty. Leila had chubby thighs, dainty long fingers and fingernails, and thick, brown hair—all signs of her growth and health in the womb for almost nine months. I was so proud to be her mom, and Jonny and I poured out our love upon our precious baby. We put a diaper on her, even though she wouldn't need it; we dressed her; we cradled her in our arms; and we covered her face with kisses. Her cheeks were so soft.

Ben came to meet his baby sister later that afternoon, so curious to see her. He eventually gained the confidence to hold her, proudly sitting up very straight and holding his arms out just as we had shown him. Jonny wrote to friends: "For just a brief moment we felt like a family of four, in body at least, of three in soul." The sadness filling the room was punctuated by moments of joy; we got to see the baby we were so curious about for the past nine months. With family all living far away, we FaceTimed with each of them to 'introduce' our Leila.

The kind nurses in the hospital never rushed us. We cherished our time with her, choosing to spend two days in the hospital, staying overnight. Throughout the night, Jonny and I alternated between holding Leila and putting her in the cold crib, especially designed for stillborn babies to preserve their deteriorating bodies as long as possible. Despite being exhausted after labor, I remember fighting sleep, not wanting to miss a moment with my child, to whom I would soon have to say good-bye. If ever I had wanted to slow down time, it was now. But of course the hours ticked mercilessly by, the moment of departure creeping ever closer.

Parents are meant to leave a labor and delivery suite with a baby strapped into a car seat, balloons and bags in tow. But we had to leave our daughter behind and turn our backs on her, knowing we would never feel the weight of her in our arms again, nor see that perfect little face this side of heaven. How do you say goodbye to your child and physically force yourself to walk away? As I held her for the very last time, Jonny kissed her on the forehead and said, "My sweet, sweet Leila, we'll see you on the other side." And then I placed my baby in the arms of a nurse whose name I don't remember, and we walked away with empty arms, past parents with their babies strapped into car seats, balloons and bags in tow.

LIFE WITHOUT LEILA

We returned to a home filled with painful reminders of Leila's absence: newborn clothes washed and folded, a Moses basket beside our bed, packets of diapers, and swaddling wraps. So many spaces and items were ready to be filled with a baby but instead remained untouched and empty. A friend came to collect the Moses basket so that we wouldn't have to stare at its unused mattress, and I passed on diapers and newborn essentials to another pregnant friend. A few days later my milk came in—another cruel reminder—as my body urged me to feed a baby who wasn't there. After days of cold compresses and painful engorgement, the milk dried up. From fullness to emptiness once again.

The days blurred together, and the effort of doing anything normal like showering, changing out of pajamas, or taking Ben to preschool left us completely drained. It felt like we were functioning in a dream state. We pressed on, weary and devastated, just doing the next thing—eating food people brought us, caring for Ben, finding a burial ground, choosing an outfit for Leila to wear in her tiny, white coffin. As the days rolled by, bringing no relief to our broken hearts and exhausted bodies, we looked to the days stretching ahead and wondered what life would now be like—life without our Leila.

> *For then this waking eye could see*
> *In many a vain vagary,*
> *The things that never were to be,*
> *Imaginations airy;*
> *Fond hopes that mothers cherish,*
> *Like still-born babes to perish.*
>
> "A Mother's Lament"
> James Montgomery

2

The Everlasting Arms

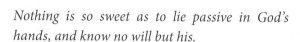

Nothing is so sweet as to lie passive in God's hands, and know no will but his.

Charles Spurgeon

LIFE BEFORE THE LOSS

Eight and a half years before Leila died, Jonny and I were married on a blue-sky summer day in Sydney, Australia. We were surrounded by family and friends, the scent of eucalyptus, and kookaburras looking on merrily. Like all newlyweds, we were blissfully ignorant of the sorrows that lay ahead of us. Eighteen months later we moved to Cambridge, England, for Jonny to complete a PhD, and where I got a job as a fourth-grade teacher. After a few happy years, we felt like it was time to grow our family.

In all honesty, I didn't feel excited at the prospect of being a mom. I struggled to picture what it would be like because it felt so abstract. I was never one to swoon over other people's newborn babies and always felt awkward when a miniature human was passed into my arms. So when I became pregnant the very first month of trying to conceive, it came as a complete shock. I cried while holding the positive test, and they weren't tears of joy. I felt unprepared and completely overwhelmed. It took a couple of months to feel the excitement grow, but when I saw the perfect profile of my baby's face during the first ultrasound, I was smitten. As my belly grew, I felt him somersaulting in my womb, and I couldn't wait to meet my first child. The rest of the pregnancy passed uneventfully, and our son Benjamin was born on August 18, 2012.

When he turned one, we decided it was time to try for another child. I approached the prospect of another baby very differently. I loved being a mom and savored the time I had been able to spend with Ben during his first year of life. I couldn't wait for him to have a sibling! I was so surprised when I didn't become pregnant during the first few months of trying, having assumed that it would happen just as quickly as it did the first time. After six months, I started to feel a little worried, until the local GP reassured me that up to a year of trying to conceive was "normal." When Ben turned two, I felt deflated and tired from twelve months of disappointment. Friends who had children of a similar age to Ben were all making their second pregnancy announcements, and I watched other families grow while ours remained the same. As we entered a second year of trying to conceive, we started medical investigations into what might be the problem. "Secondary infertility," they said, and then added "unexplained" when tests didn't reveal any obvious problems.

After two years of barrenness, I was feeling worn out by the experience. It certainly made me more grateful than ever for Ben, knowing I had taken him for granted, especially when I first became pregnant. Jonny and I were convicted over how we had treated God like a vending machine, letting him know when we were ready to have children, and presuming that he would give them to us when we decided it was time. We prayed a lot more earnestly during this season, crying out to the Lord for him to open my womb, knowing that it was only by his hand that the miracle of new life began. Prayerful as we were, it felt like my womb was firmly closed. We hadn't given up hope, but we certainly weren't feeling expectant. As Ben approached his third birthday, two years since we started trying to conceive again, I wondered if he would ever have a brother or sister.

Then, one morning, I woke up early to take a pregnancy test and saw the two lines confirming the good news we had been longing for. This time, instead of tears of fear and trepidation, I cried tears of relief and gratitude. God had given us another child! I didn't need to wait for the first ultrasound to feel connected to this child— I was instantly bonded. A few days after the positive test I cycled into the city center, with Ben on his booster seat behind me, thinking, "I'm carrying *two* children on this bike!" What bliss! Each ultrasound was wondrous, and I watched this baby kick and wriggle on the screen for as long as they would allow. I was relieved to get past the twenty-week scan with no red flags or developmental anomalies spotted. We were all clear! Now we just had to wait for this little one's arrival in the spring.

But then came the six words that changed everything. They echoed in my ears, crushed my hopes, and broke my heart.

"I'm sorry. There is no heartbeat."

The joy I had felt at the gift of a longed-for child—a daughter!—suddenly drained out of me. The light that filled my world when my daughter was alive was extinguished. Thomas Smyth, a man who experienced the death of three of his children, captures it exactly:

"O Death! Thou art the destroyer of a mother's bliss."[1]

RESTING IN THE ARMS

When the sonographer confirmed Leila's death, the bottom of my world gave way and I felt like I was in free fall. I tried to steady myself by curling up in bed with a hot water bottle and lying still. But of course, this didn't stop the feeling of falling. The news of my daughter's death had split apart the foundation upon which I stood. Every night, I cried on and off until morning without restraint; from whimpering to anguished groaning—even wailing. I sounded the way I felt, like I was plummeting into a bottomless cavern.

In the midst of this dark despair, a friend sent me Deuteronomy 33:27: "The eternal God is your dwelling place, and underneath are the everlasting arms." For just a moment, stillness replaced the feeling of free fall. As I lay in my bedroom, crying like I'd never cried before, God's Word assured me that I wasn't in fact falling deeper and deeper into a bottomless pit. I was being held by the everlasting arms of my heavenly Father. Theodore Cuyler, a man whose two infant children and one adult daughter died, writes:

> One great purpose in all affliction is to bring
> us down to the everlasting arms. What new
> strength and peace it gives us to feel them
> underneath us! We know that, as far as we may
> have sunk, we cannot go any farther.[2]

There was only one pair of arms that could hold me
through the worst moment of my life—the everlasting
arms of an eternal God. That verse from my friend comforted me with the truth that I could lean the full weight
of my sorrow into strong arms, which would never tire
or let me go. There was no grief too heavy for them.

BELIEVING IN THE DARKNESS

Even though Deuteronomy 33:27 brought me comfort,
there were still many times when I didn't *feel* like it was
true, especially in the raw, early days of loss. Often, I still
felt like I was free-falling in the dark. But early on in my
suffering I came to a crossroads where I had to decide:
Am I going to keep believing what I know about God,
despite my circumstances tempting me to feel otherwise?

Many Christians before us have had to wrestle with
the same dilemma, including a missionary woman
named Lilias Trotter. She was born in 1853 to a privi-
leged family in London, England. She had a successful
career as a painter but gave it up to share the gospel
with the people of Algeria in North Africa. Her mission
work was fruitful, but she also experienced many dis-
couraging periods where she wondered what God was
doing. During one hard season that lasted for years, her
work was almost completely shut down. In her diary,

dated August 10, 1901, she wrote, "Believe in the darkness what you have seen in the light."[3] As Lilias looked around her, life was bleak. Was God still there? It didn't feel like it. Was he still working all things together for good? It didn't look like it. Did his steadfast love really endure forever? God's love felt cold and distant. At that moment Lilias made a choice. Instead of stumbling around in the darkness, doubting everything she had believed, she chose to believe in the darkness what she had seen in the light.

When Leila died, I entered a very low place where my feelings threatened to override my faith. Everything I had ever known about God was being shaken by the tragic death of my longed-for daughter. My friend's text with Deuteronomy 33:27 encouraged me to keep believing in the darkness what I had seen in the light, even when—especially when—it didn't *feel* true. God's arms were underneath me every moment of every dark day. His arms held me. They will hold you too.

O how sweet to walk in this pilgrim way,
   Leaning on the Everlasting Arms!
O how bright the path grows from day to day,
   Leaning on the Everlasting Arms!

What have I to dread, what have I to fear,
   Leaning on the Everlasting Arms!
I have peace complete with my Lord so near,
   Leaning on the Everlasting Arms!

Elisha Hoffman

3

Man of Sorrows

The path in which we follow Him—is bedewed with His tears and stained with His blood.

Edward Payson

ALONE IN GRIEF

Grieving the death of your baby often feels lonely. Everyone who has experienced the death of a loved one will recall the comments people make that reveal a lack of understanding. A well-meaning woman at church declared that I would have twin girls in the future, while another said that God would give me a healthy baby next time. Four months after Leila was stillborn, I had to visit the same hospital for routine tests. Returning there was triggering for me, and during the checkup, a phlebotomist asked why I was crying. When I told her the reason, she replied abruptly, "Four months is a long time," implying that I should have moved on by now. Not only did these comments hurt, but they made me feel alone in a sea of grief surrounded by people who just didn't get it.

I naturally gravitated toward mothers who had similar stories to mine, who knew what it felt like to hear, "There is no heartbeat." I am grateful to the Lord for bringing them into my life during this time. And yet, my journey could still feel lonely. Their stories were different from mine, as were the nuances of their grief. Their baby was not Leila, their valley was not my valley, and their path through grief was not my path.

The person who best understood what I was going through was my husband. We were both parents whose daughter died. He was the only other person who was there for the pronouncement of death and who witnessed the deathly silence of Leila's birth. Jonny's grief was as deep and wide as my own, and together we experienced the loss of our daughter. Yet even in our shared loss, our grief was different. Only I knew what it was like to house a baby in my own body, to experience the uncomfortable and wondrous changes of pregnancy. Only I knew the feeling of regular movement and then the sudden stillness of no movement. I wondered if my own body had somehow caused my daughter's death. Only I knew the pain of labor—pushing this baby, who was still physically joined to me, into the world. As much as he tried, Jonny could never fully understand these unique experiences of a mother. Just as I couldn't completely understand the layers of his grief as a father.

A few months after Leila's death, Jonny and I met with a doctor who had spent many years working as a neonatologist consultant and was kindly helping us process elements of her stillbirth. In response to our tearful questions, he said something I'll never forget:

Suffering is not a question that demands an answer. It is not a problem that requires a solution. It is a mystery that needs a presence.[1]

I realized then that what I needed was a companion who knew what sorrow felt like, what *my* sorrow felt like. I needed someone who would be present with me in every part of my suffering. I needed Emmanuel—God with us. I needed Jesus.

TEARS BY A TOMB

Until Leila died, I didn't know I had such a large reservoir of tears. Some days I thought I would never stop crying; the tears didn't dry up. One of the sweetest blessings was when friends or family visited and simply cried with me and Jonny, their tears declaring that our daughter's death was something worth mourning. How much sweeter it was to know that in the presence of death, tears rolled down the face of my Savior.

The moment is recorded for us in John's gospel. In chapter 11, Jesus travels to Bethany where his friend Lazarus has been dead for four days. This isn't a shock to Jesus; he has just told his disciples plainly, "Lazarus has died." Not only this, but he knows that he will soon raise his friend from the grave saying, "I go to awaken him" (John 11:11). With his sovereign foreknowledge, Jesus knows that this story has a happy ending, which makes his emotional response even more surprising:

> When Mary reached the place where Jesus was and saw him, she fell at his feet and said, "Lord, if you had been here, my brother would not have died."

> When Jesus saw her weeping, and the Jews
> who had come along with her also weeping,
> he was deeply moved in spirit and troubled.
> "Where have you laid him?" he asked.
> "Come and see, Lord," they replied.
> Jesus wept. (John 11:32–35 NIV)

When Jesus sees Mary and the others weeping, he is deeply moved by what John Calvin calls "the common misery of the human race."[2] Sin, which had entered the world and left its deathly stain over everything, makes our Lord indignant with anger. He understands the truth that death is a terrible enemy. So when he comes to the place where his friend Lazarus is buried, and when he sees the tears of Mary and the other mourners, Jesus weeps. It is the shortest verse in the Bible, but those two words reveal so much about the tender heart of our Savior. John Eadie, a nineteenth-century theologian, says, "There was no attempt to drown His sympathies, and force Himself into a hard and inhuman indifference. Neither was He ashamed of His possession of our ordinary sensibilities. He felt it no weakness to weep in public."[3] When I cried painful tears for my daughter after she died, Jesus knew just what that felt like, and perfectly so.

FRIEND IN GRIEF

As comforting as I found this, Jesus's tears were not the only reason he could sympathize with me in my suffering. It is one thing to cry at the suffering seen around you; it is quite another to be the one who suffers. Yes, Jesus shed tears. But more importantly, he shed his own blood. Jesus knows better than anyone

what it feels like to suffer, and that is why he is our closest friend in grief.

We see his life of suffering edge toward its climax in
the garden of Gethsemane. Matthew's gospel recounts,
"Then [Jesus] said to them, 'My soul is very sorrow-
ful, even to death; remain here, and watch with me'"
(Matthew 26:38). And Luke's gospel: "being in agony
he prayed more earnestly; and his sweat became like
great drops of blood falling down to the ground" (Luke
22:44). We know that sorrow is immensely physical;
we feel it in our chest, our stomach, our shoulders, our
heads, our faces. It changes how we stand, how we lie
down, how we walk. And here in Gethsemane we see
Jesus taking on the physical gamut of agony, his sweat
dripping from his brow like drops of blood.

In the days after Leila's death, waiting for her stillbirth, I felt the strongest sense of dread I have ever
experienced. At the time, I remember thinking about
Jesus in the garden the night before his crucifixion, as
the moment of his death drew ever closer. He wrestled
with his Father in prayer, agonizing over what he was
about to go through. I thought, "If I feel this terrified
with what *I* am about to go through, how much more
terrifying must it have been for *Jesus* with what lay
ahead for him?"

Jesus's life of suffering, his tears and agony, is cap-
tured by Isaiah the prophet in that most memorable of
chapters—Isaiah 53:

> He was despised and rejected by men,
>   a man of sorrows and acquainted with grief
> and as one from whom men hide their faces
>   he was despised, and we esteemed him not.

> Surely he has borne our griefs
>   and carried our sorrows;
> yet we esteemed him stricken,
>   smitten by God, and afflicted. (Isaiah 53:3–4)

What a bittersweet description of the one who is acquainted with every facet of our grief: "man of sorrows." Jesus did not receive the title because he was a man who merely knew what it was to cry; he was a man of sorrows because he truly knew what it was to suffer. Edward Payson writes,

> His sufferings, instead of being less, were incomparably greater than they appeared to be. No finite mind can conceive of their extent; nor was any of the human race ever so well entitled to the appellation of *the Man of Sorrows*—as the man Christ Jesus. His sufferings began with his birth, and ended but with his life.[4]

There was not one part of my suffering that Jesus couldn't understand. He could walk with me through my deepest sorrows because he was the ultimate sufferer, the truest man of sorrows that has ever walked upon the earth. Jesus's suffering led him all the way to the cross. As the following verse in Isaiah says, "But he was pierced for our transgressions; he was crushed for our iniquities; upon him was the chastisement that brought us peace, and with his wounds we are healed" (Isaiah 53:5).

In those three terrifying days and nights between Leila's death and stillbirth, I felt like I was seeing Jesus through new eyes. I had never seen him so clearly on the path ahead, carrying his cross, enduring the worst suffering of any human before or after, crying out in his darkest moment, "My God, my God, why have you forsaken me?" (Matthew 27:46), and receiving no answer. The light of the world alone in the darkness! As I lay in bed feeling the terror of what lay ahead, tears streaming down my face, I experienced the presence of Jesus, the Man of Sorrows. I had a companion in my grief who would be with me in my darkest moment. I didn't feel lonely anymore as I entered the valley of the shadow of death. Hallelujah! What a Savior!

> *"Man of Sorrows," what a name*
> *for the Son of God who came*
> *ruined sinners to reclaim!*
> *Hallelujah! What a Savior!*
>
> Philip P. Bliss

4

Written in His Book

~

Nothing takes place save according to his appointment.

John Calvin

WHAT IF . . . ?

If you're anything like me, you have replayed the days
before your child's death in vivid detail, wondering
what you could have done to prevent it. Even today,
seven years later, those thoughts can still haunt me. I
remember going to an appointment with my midwife
only a week before Leila's death, and she asked me if
the baby's movements had been normal. I recall hesitat-
ing slightly. I hadn't really thought about it. Throughout my entire pregnancy no one had ever asked me to
count kicks or consciously monitor movements. When
the midwife listened to Leila's heartbeat briefly, I wish I
had asked her to listen for longer and compare the heart
rate to the last time she had recorded it. Had it slowed
down? Were there any red flags? Could I have changed
the outcome if I had paid closer attention?

When I phoned the hospital concerned about reduced movements the day before Leila died, the nurse encouraged me to stay home and count kicks. I lay on my side and waited for a very long time before I finally felt some reassuring movements. But as I look back, I know it shouldn't have taken that long for Leila to move. Retrospectively, I realize that her movements were weaker than normal. How I wish I had ignored the nurse's advice and driven straight to the hospital! Maybe they could have acted quickly—taken Leila out and given her vital medical care. If I had been more decisive, could I have saved my baby's life? I wonder if similar questions have kept you awake at night.

Thomas Boston, an eighteenth-century Scottish theologian who experienced the death of six of his children, said that when we turn these hard moments over and over in our minds, viewing them from all sides and obsessively considering all the different possible causes, we end up "in a foam and a fret,"[1] tossed about in a sea of instability. My "what if" questions threatened to consume me, making me feel guilty and close to despair. The only way out of the "foam and fret" was for me to stop looking inward at myself, and instead shift my gaze upward. Thomas Boston gives good advice: "Lift up your eyes toward heaven, *see the doing of God* in it, the operation of his hand: look at that, and consider it well; eye the first cause of the crook in your lot; behold how it is *the work of God,* his *doing.*"[2] How could I find peace when the "what ifs" of my loss replayed over and over in my mind? I could look upward to heaven, to the sovereign God who ordains whatsoever comes to pass.

WHATSOEVER...

In answer to the question, "What could we have done differently?" God's word is clear: *nothing*. Psalm 139 tells us that our babies' days were numbered before they came into being:

> Your eyes saw my unformed substance;
> in your book were written, every one of them,
>   the days that were formed for me,
>   when as yet there was none of them.
>
> (Psalm 139:16)

This means that our babies were only ever going to live for the days that God apportioned to them. On the one-year anniversary of Leila's birth, I couldn't help imagining what the day might have been like had things turned out differently: What would she look like as a one-year-old? How long would her hair be? What kind of cake would I have baked for her? But the fact is, she was never going to have a first birthday on earth. She was never going to open her eyes outside the womb; she was never going to utter a sound; she was never going to smile at her parents or brother. Her clothes were never going to be worn; her milk was never going to be drunk; her bed was never going to be slept in. She was never going to crawl or cry or laugh. Before God knit Leila together in my womb, he ordained that her life was only for the womb—about 277 days. Nothing I could have done would have altered the eternal plans of God, even though I have often longed to go back in time and give it a try.

Not only were the length of our babies' days written before their conception, God's hand was also upon them for their whole lives, however short. David writes in Psalm 139:

> You hem me in, behind and before,
>   and lay your hand upon me. (v. 5)
> If I take the wings of the morning
>   and dwell in the uttermost parts of the sea,
> even there your hand shall lead me,
>   and your right hand shall hold me. (vv. 9–10)

What is true for David is true for all of God's people. Our babies were hemmed in by God, behind and before. He led them and he held them, and nothing happened by accident. They could go nowhere without God's hand leading them, even unto death. "God has by an eternal decree, immovable as mountains of brass (Zechariah 6:1), appointed the whole of everyone's lot, the crooked parts thereof, as well as the straight."[3] This is true for our lives, and it is true for the lives of our children.

Imagine living in a world in which God isn't in control, as many people believe, a world that operates according to random fate instead of sovereign appointment. In this world, some are lucky and some are not. In our case, we were the "unfortunate" ones whose babies "just happened" to die—another sad statistic. If we live this way, then life will be an anxious, white-knuckled ride in which we hold our breath and hope that fate won't deal us a bad hand—fingers crossed, touch wood! Instead, as believers we can say with Job, in the midst of devastating loss, that our God:

Is unchangeable, and who can turn him back?
  What he desires, that he does.
For he will complete what he appoints for me,
  and many such things are in his mind.

(Job 23:13–14)

Even though it is mercifully uncommon now, when I do lie in bed replaying the events surrounding Leila's death, I have learned to surrender those memories to a sovereign God "who from all eternity, did, by the most wise and holy counsel of His own will, freely, and unchangeably ordain whatsoever comes to pass."[4] When I realize that I could not have saved my daughter's life, peace flows into my heart, and I sleep more soundly. Leila's days were written in God's book before she came into being. It was God's appointment, and so I leave it with him.

Whate'er my God ordains is right,
Here shall my stand be taken;
Though sorrow, need, or death be mine,
Yet I am not forsaken.
My Father's care is round me there;
He holds me that I shall not fall,
And so to Him I leave it all.

Samuel Rodigast

5

Things Too Wonderful for Me

❧

When we cannot trace God's hand, we can trust God's heart.

Charles Spurgeon

ASKING QUESTIONS

Knowing that Leila's death didn't happen by chance but by divine decree, brought me a large measure of peace. Having confidence that her days were numbered before she came into being, freed me from asking, "What if . . . ?" Yet I was still left with questions about the God who ordained the death of my baby.

A few weeks after Leila's death and stillbirth, a friend gave birth to a healthy baby boy in the same hospital. All the preparations they made for his arrival turned out to be worthwhile; he was brought home to a house of rejoicing, while only a few streets away was our house of mourning. God planned for one baby to be delivered safely into the world, and for another baby to die a week before her due date. I felt like God had been kind to that family and cruel to ours. How should we understand it when two very different providences come from the same God—just streets away? Is the God who wrote such a small number beside my daughter's days *really* good?

GOD IS GOOD

It doesn't take long to search the Scriptures to see how they answer this question: "Good and upright is the LORD" (Psalm 25:8); he "is righteous in all his ways and kind in all his works" (Psalm 145:17); "you are good and do good" (Psalm 119:68). Other psalms declare: "Oh give thanks to the LORD, for he is good, for his steadfast love endures forever!" (Psalms 106; 107; 118; 136). The Bible is clear. God is good, and so are his plans; we cannot detach his decrees from his character.

It is tempting to try to define God's character by our experience. When life is easy, we have no problem believing God is good. We feel God's face shining upon us in kindness, and it is easy to rejoice in him. But when hard things come our way, our feelings change. We start to call into question all we thought we knew about God, and it's tempting to throw accusations of cruelty at him. It has been a hard fight for Jonny and me to keep believing in God's goodness through the valley of Leila's death. There have been days when we have doubted and even denied that God is good. A few years after Leila's death, we went through another season of hardship with our son's adoption, and I remember how quickly we accused God of being unkind toward us—again. When God gave us good gifts, we were full of praise; but as soon as we felt them being pried from our fingers, we were quick to complain, "How could you,

Lord?" Abraham Kuyper explored this dilemma in his book *To Be Near unto God,* in which he uses the example of a mother whose child has died:

> How could a loving God cruelly cast her down from the heights of her great happiness into the depths of bereavement and woe? In perplexity of grief her language becomes that of despair and of defiant unbelief. "Speak no more of God to me. Cruelty can not be love. There is no God." And so the break of happiness in life becomes the break of faith in God. She thought that she knew the Lord. Now that he shows himself in a different way from what she had imagined, she abandons all she ever believed.[1]

I can relate to this woman's struggle and wrestling. I too went from the heights of happiness (a positive pregnancy test!) to the depths of woe ("I'm sorry. There is no heartbeat."). But despite my feelings, I was called to keep believing that God is good. Why? Because it is true. Just like it is true that the moon is always round, even when we can't see all of it. Some nights we can see a bright, full moon glowing in the sky, undeniably round. But on other nights we can only see a half moon, or a crescent moon; or maybe the moon is completely obscured from sight. But what we see doesn't change the fact that the moon is always round.[2] After Leila died, I didn't *feel* like God was good, but by his grace I tried to trust his infallible Word that assured me that he *is* good, even when I couldn't see it.

Of course, it is still very hard to accept God's goodness as you stare at an empty crib and give away the newborn diapers you bought; as you ache to hold your baby just one more time (or for the first time). Our finite minds cannot comprehend how a good God can ordain suffering, especially when our arms are empty. God is good, yes, but sometimes mysteriously so.

LEARNING NOT TO UNDERSTAND

Job was a man who had to live in the tension of this mystery. After facing unimaginable suffering—the loss of all his possessions, his health, and even his ten children—he too had questions for God and feelings like ours. Speaking to God, he said:

> I cry to you for help and you do not answer me;
>   I stand, and you only look at me.
> You have turned cruel to me;
>   with the might of your hand you persecute me.
> You lift me up on the wind; you make me ride
>   on it,
>   and you toss me about in the roar of the
>   storm. (Job 30:20–22)

It is not hard to relate to Job's words! God's hand in our suffering does feel cruel. We feel caught up in a whirlwind, tossed about in a storm by the very hand of God. And sometimes when we pray, God remains silent. Like us, Job longed for answers: "Let the Almighty answer me!" (Job 31:35). He wanted his suffering to be explained in full; not by his friends who were full of error and accusation, but by the God who ultimately stood behind it. Just like Job, we want an audience with God, an opportunity to ask him to explain himself: "Why did you plan for my baby to die?" But as Job discovered, an audience with the Almighty can be a terrifying experience.[3] Because when we come before the Creator God, we are completely laid bare.

After all of Job's questioning and pleading for answers, God answered him, but not in the way he expected. God had some questions for him:

> Where were you when I laid the foundation of
> the earth?
> Tell me, if you have understanding.
> Who determined its measurements—surely
> you know!
> Or who stretched the line upon it? . . .
> Have you commanded the morning since your
> days began,
> and caused the dawn to know its place, . . .
> Have you entered into the springs of the sea,
> or walked in the recesses of the deep? . . .
> Have you entered the storehouses of the snow,
> or have you seen the storehouses of the hail . . . ?
> (Job 38:4–5, 12, 16, 22)

In my darkest days of grief, the Lord brought these verses to my mind. They reminded me that my understanding of the world was limited, especially my understanding of why my daughter died. They reminded me that I was a small, finite creature made by a big, infinite Creator whose ways were far above mine. Just like Job, my questions and accusations were ultimately "without knowledge" (Job 38:2). God alone is the one with perfect knowledge and command of all things: from the drops of dew to clusters of stars, from clouds in the sky to dust on the earth, from mountain goats to hawks and eagles—and yes, even to my baby in the womb, to whom he said, "Thus far you shall come and no further."

When Job was confronted with God in all his fathomless knowledge, his questions dissolved:

> Behold, I am of small account; what shall I
> answer you?
> I lay my hand on my mouth. (Job 40:4)

> Therefore I have uttered what I did not
> understand,
> things too wonderful for me, which I did not
> know. (Job 42:3)

John J. Murray writes: "It was when Job was willing not to understand that he began to understand."[4] The same is true for us. If we are waiting for all our questions to be answered this side of heaven, then we will be left wanting. If we are trying to work out how we could have made things turn out differently, then we will be fretful and exhausted. If we are striving to understand what only God knows, then we will be constantly restless. How could a good God ordain for my daughter Leila to die? I don't know. Like Job, I must be willing not to understand and to leave it in the hands of a God who does, a God who is "righteous in all his ways and kind in all his works" (Psalm 145:17)—albeit sometimes mysteriously so.

> *Judge not the Lord by feeble sense,*
> *But trust Him for His grace;*
> *Behind a frowning providence*
> *He hides a smiling face.*

His purposes will ripen fast,
Unfolding every hour;
The bud may have a bitter taste,
But sweet will be the flow'r.

Blind unbelief is sure to err
And scan His work in vain;
God is His own interpreter,
And He will make it plain.

William Cowper

6

Precious in His Sight

~

Because every baby carves a path across its mother's heart, from the moment she dares to glance up at the bathroom mirror and catch her own eyes there, King Solomon's eyes, telling her she is responsible for another life. Two hearts beat inside her. There is a space traveler criss-crossing the universe within her . . . making itself the center of her interior cosmos.

Nora Seton

DISPOSABLE?

It is hard to imagine how our secular culture could have a lower view of life in the womb than it does right now. When I was pregnant with our first son, Ben, I'll never forget my GP informing me of my "options." When you visit abortion-provider websites, you will likely not find any terms that describe the baby as a human person in various stages of development. Instead, they use the depersonalized language of "health care services" and "fundamental human rights" to make it more palatable to women considering abortion. The closest they get is referring to "the pregnancy." Which begs the question: pregnant *with what*? Our society wants to make it as easy as possible for women to end the life of their baby at any stage of development, without having to think too much about it.

WONDERS IN THE WOMB

The wonders of science have taught us so much about the value of life in the womb. At the point of conception, before implantation in the mother's uterus, the two parents' chromosomes combine to create a unique and complete genetic code that will not change throughout the course of that human life. At five weeks (two weeks after fertilization), a tiny, intricate heart starts beating. At six weeks, a nose, mouth, and ears start to take shape, and the intestines and brains begin to develop. At seven weeks, the hands and feet start to form, and the baby might start to move. At weeks ten and eleven, fingernails grow, and the baby starts to kick, stretch, and hiccup. At twelve weeks, a baby has his or her own unique set of fingerprints, and a baby girl's ovaries will contain more than two million eggs. Between fifteen to twenty weeks, babies will sense light; their skeletons will harden to bone; and they will start to hear sound, including the voice of their mother.[1]

While the abortion industry tries to deny it, science has shown us many of the wonders of life in the womb: a complex human being beginning life at conception and continuing to develop throughout the pregnancy. But science alone is limited. "As you do not know the way the spirit comes to the bones in the womb of a woman with child, so you do not know the work of God who makes everything" (Ecclesiastes 11:5). Without the illumination of God's Word, people will draw all sorts of conclusions to demean the personhood of a baby in the womb. Some argue strongly that life does not start until implantation in the womb. Others believe that human life begins when the umbilical cord is cut, since now, severed from its mother, the baby has become an "independent" being. Some suggest humanness begins when the mother can feel the baby move in the womb, or when the child takes its first breath on its own. Francis Crick, who discovered the structure of DNA, said that a newborn baby should only be declared "human" when it has passed certain tests in the days following birth![2]

How would people who hold such views make sense of the grief of a mother whose baby dies in the womb? How would they explain the tears shed for someone they don't consider to be human? Whether your baby died at four weeks or thirty-nine weeks in the womb, you grieved the death of a person who was very special to you. Scripture, not science, is ultimately the place where our sorrow over their death is explained. We weep over the death of our little ones because they are valuable, as God's Word affirms.

CREATION IN THE WOMB

Our babies had dignity from the moment of conception because they were made by God:

> You formed my inward parts;
>   you knitted me together in my mother's
>   womb.

I praise you, for I am fearfully and wonder-
    fully made.
Wonderful are your works;
    my soul knows it very well.
My frame was not hidden from you,
when I was being made in secret,
    intricately woven in the depths of the earth.
                                    (Psalm 139:13–15)

The Hebrew verb "woven" in verse 15 means to "weave" or "embroider." This word is only used nine times in the Old Testament, and all other uses outside of Psalm 139 are connected to the embroidery work at the tabernacle. For example, Moses uses it to speak of the work of weaving cherubim onto the veil that separated the Holy Place from the Most Holy Place (Exodus 26:36). Given its limited use and narrow focus, clearly the verb is intimately connected to the holy things of God: in Exodus, the weaving together of fabrics used in the tabernacle; in Psalm 139, the weaving together of a child in the womb. It doesn't matter at what point during the pregnancy your baby died, how developed they were, or whether or not they had medical complications. They were still image-bearing, soul-possessing human beings whom the God of the universe intimately wove together, and therefore they are precious in his sight—*holy* precious.

PERSONHOOD IN THE WOMB

Some might think that Scripture's view of the unborn baby is a bit hazy, that it doesn't really comment on life in the womb. But this is far from true! The Bible speaks of many people before their birth, and, in each case, they are referred to as real people with personhood and dignity. Notice these examples:

Jacob and Esau

> And the LORD said to [Rebekah], "Two nations are in your womb, and two peoples from within you shall be divided; the one shall be stronger than the other, the older shall serve the younger" (Genesis 25:23).[3]

Jacob

> In the womb *he took his brother by the heel*, and in his manhood he strove with God (Hosea 12:3).

Samson

> Then the woman came and told her husband, "A man of God came to me, and his appearance was like the appearance of the angel of God, very awesome . . . . he said to me, 'Behold, you shall conceive and bear *a son*. So then drink no wine or strong drink, and eat nothing unclean, *for the child shall be a Nazirite to God from the womb to the day of his death*'" (Judges 13:6–7).

David

> Yet you are he who *took me from the womb*; you made me trust you at my mother's breasts. On you was I cast from my birth, and *from my mother's womb you have been my God* (Psalm 22:9–10).

> Behold, I was brought forth in iniquity, *and in sin did my mother conceive me* (Psalm 51:5).

The Servant of the Lord

> Listen to me, O coastlands, and give attention, you peoples from afar. *The LORD called me from the womb, from the body of my mother he named my name* . . . . And now the LORD says, *he who formed me from the womb to be his servant,* to bring Jacob back to him; and that Israel might be gathered to him—for I am honored in the eyes of the LORD, and my God has become my strength" (Isaiah 49:1, 5).

Jeremiah

> Now the word of the LORD came to me, saying, *"Before I formed you in the womb I knew you, and before you were born I consecrated you*; I appointed you a prophet to the nations" (Jeremiah 1:4–5).

John the Baptist

> For he will be great before the Lord. And he must not drink wine or strong drink, and he will be filled with the Holy Spirit, *even from his mother's womb* (Luke 1:15).

Jesus

> And behold, you will *conceive in your womb and bear a son,* and you shall call his name Jesus (Luke 1:31).

> And at the end of eight days, when he was circumcised, he was called Jesus, *the name given by the angel before he was conceived in the womb* (Luke 2:21).

As you can see from this long list of examples, none of these people became human beings at some point during pregnancy, or after birth. They are indiscriminately spoken of with pronouns and personhood from conception, through life in the womb, to life after birth.[4]

As I write this, I am aware that some of you reading this book may carry around the painful memory of an abortion in your past. When you hear about the personhood of a baby in the womb from conception, the feelings that dominate your heart may be guilt, shame, and regret. You might even be wondering if a subsequent miscarriage or stillbirth is a punishment for your past choice. The layers of your emotions are understandably complex, but I pray that you would know deep in your heart this wonderful, liberating truth from God's Word: "There is therefore no condemnation for those who are in Christ Jesus" (Romans 8:1). Your recent miscarriage or stillbirth may be a sore providence from God, but it is not a sin punishment from him. His forgiveness is full and free.

OUR BABIES IN THE WOMB

At Leila's funeral, Jonny delivered a twenty-minute eulogy about our daughter. After the service a friend wrote to him admitting that when he saw "eulogy" on the order of service, he wondered what on earth Jonny was going to say about a baby who only lived in the womb, and whom people never got to meet. After hearing the eulogy, he said he understood why Jonny spoke for twenty minutes about his stillborn daughter—even though her life was short, she was someone worth talking about. She was our beloved Leila, and she had a profound impact on our family. Jonny told everyone gathered there that day all about her: about the happy day we found out we were pregnant, her somersaults in the womb, her dark head of hair, her nose like her brother's, her lovely soft skin, and how her fingers would curl around ours, even in death. There has never been, and never will be, another baby like our Leila Judith Grace.

I'm sure you feel the same way about your baby. He or she is one of a kind. Sadly, our surrounding culture does not honor their worth. Have you been made to feel like your tears are unwarranted, or that your grief is out of proportion to your loss? Well, God's Word tells us otherwise. It makes sense of the sorrow you feel about the death of your baby—a baby who was fearfully and wonderfully made, a divine creation, a *person*. Precious to us, and even more so, to God.

> *Her span was like the sky,*
> *Whose thousand stars shine beautiful and bright,*
> *Like flowers that know not what it is to die,*
> *Like long link'd shadeless months of polar light,*
> *Like music floating o'er a waveless lake,*
> *While echo answers from the flowery brake.*
>
> David MacBeth Moir

7

You Are Still a Mother

God has given me three sons, all living, only the youngest lives with God.

Oliver Heywood

I AM HER MOTHER

"How many children do you have?" is a question I am often asked. No matter how many times I have heard it, it can still raise my heart rate and make me flustered. Sometimes I still hesitate. Should I just say, "three," since that is how many I have on earth? What if they ask their ages? Then I will have to explain that my daughter died . . . . But laying aside someone else's potential discomfort, there is only one answer that sits right with me: "Four. I have four children." My mother's heart cannot leave out my second child. I am her mother.

Recently I took my three-year-old to the children's hospital ER. After about three hours of waiting, a nurse came out and called for the next child in a loud voice: "Leila!" Instinctively I thought she was calling us; she was calling my daughter's name. Within a second or two reality set in, as I watched a different little girl with her mother walk toward the nurse. But hearing that name made my heart leap—my daughter! I am her mother.

One of the hardest things about the death of a baby is that you have nothing to show for your motherhood. After saying goodbye to Leila, we came home from the hospital, and I folded up all the baby clothes I had washed and put them away. Then I gave away the newborn diapers and baby wipes I had bought. One of the most agonizing experiences was having my milk come in a few days after her stillbirth. My body was still providing for my baby, responding to the hormonal triggers following labor, urging me to feed a newborn who was not there and who did not need my milk. Almost as hard as the milk coming was the milk drying up. And yet everything in me still yearned for my baby. I am her mother.

DEATH CANNOT SEVER

A live birth or a surviving child is not what makes you a mother. Since your child's life began at conception, so too did your motherhood. The death of your child does not undo that reality. We see this beautifully displayed in Luke's gospel. In a town called Nain, Jesus witnesses the funeral procession of a young man:

> As [Jesus] drew near to the gate of the town, behold, a man who had died was being carried out, *the only son of his mother*, and she was a widow, and a considerable crowd from the town was with her. (Luke 7:12)

I love the language Luke uses. The man is dead, but he is still "the only son of his mother." Death didn't sever the mother-son relationship. Luke continues:

> And when the Lord saw her, he had compassion on her and said to her, "Do not weep." Then he came up and touched the bier, and the bearers stood still. And he said, "Young man, I say to you, arise." And the dead man sat up and began to speak, *and Jesus gave him to his mother.* (Luke 7:13–15)

In life and in death, this woman is his mother. And in resurrection life, Jesus gives her back her son.

We see this again with Jairus's twelve-year-old daughter. Jesus and his disciples have just been told that the little girl has died:

> And when [Jesus] came to the house, he allowed no one to enter with him, except Peter and John and James, *and the father and mother of the child.* And all were weeping and mourning for her, but he said, "Do not weep, for she is not dead but sleeping." And they laughed at him, knowing that she was dead. But taking her by the hand he called, saying, "Child, arise." And her spirit returned, and she got up at once. And he directed that something should be given her to eat. (Luke 8:51–55)

This little girl's parents are as much her father and mother beside her deathbed as they are when she wakes up and needs food. In both examples, the expression of parenthood is different, but the reality of the parent-child relationship does not change—even in death.

MOTHERHOOD WITHOUT THEM

So what does motherhood look like for us bereaved moms when there's no baby to rock, and settle and feed—when there is no child to raise? Of course, it will look very different for each of us. I have come to appreciate that there is a particular complexity to grief that comes with a miscarriage before a baby's gender can be known. But one thing we have in common is that we all carry around our child in our hearts, our memories, and our longings. Nora Seton captures it poignantly when she writes: "The death of a baby is a melody played softly through its mother's life like an intimate dirge, and you have to have died a little yourself to hear the music."[1]

You and I carry that sad melody—the intimate dirge—around with us, and very few ever hear the music. So it can be helpful to find ways to express our motherly love for our children. For me, it means that when asked, I include Leila in the number of children I have. I am more able now to push past the awkwardness of the other person when I tell them I have a baby in heaven. We often remind Zac and Hannah that they have a big sister, and we try to help Ben remember when he met and held his little sister. Jonny does a little catechism with the kids on the Lord's Day that reminds them we're about to go to church and join Leila and the angels in worship. We have Leila's hand and footprint on display on our mantelpiece and her photo on top of the piano. Every Christmas we hang ornaments on the tree with her name on it. And when we get the opportunity, we love to visit her grave in Cambridge, England. Some of our parental love for her is expressed in caring for that little plot of land—cleaning her headstone, sowing grass seed, and planting daffodil bulbs. And every year on March 17, now called Saint Leila's Day in our home, we go out as a family and enjoy a meal in remembrance of her. Then we return home and let off yellow helium balloons into the sky, our gaze lifted heavenward, longing for that sweet reunion.

I don't get to watch Leila play sports, braid her hair, or take her out for mommy-daughter dates. How I wish I could do all those things! But I won't forget her, and I won't stop talking about her. The world may forget you are a mother to your child. Even those close to you may forget—unintentionally, they may not mention your baby's name or include him or her in a birth order. But God will not forget them. He blessed you with a baby whom he knitted together in your womb. In life, and in death, he views you as your child's mother. You are still a mother.

> *Sarah! my last, my youngest love.*
> *The crown of every other!*
> *Though thou art born in heaven above,*
> *I am thine only mother,*
> *Nor will affection let me*
> *Believe thou canst forget me.*
>
> *Then,—thou in heaven and I on earth,*
> *May this one hope delight us.*
> *That thou wilt hail my second birth,*
> *When death shall reunite us,*

Where worlds no more can sever
Parent and child for ever.

"A Mother's Lament"

James Montgomery

8

Safe in His Arms

The child has only changed a bed in the garden, and is planted up higher, nearer the sun, where he shall thrive better than in this wasteland.

Samuel Rutherford

A SAFE PLACE

We tend to think that the safest place for babies is in their mother's arms. Our maternal instinct is to hold our babies close and shelter them from harm. But hard as a mother may try, she cannot protect her baby from the dangers of this fallen world, from the serious (injury or sickness), to the less serious (a colicky stomach or a sniffly cold), to the more trivial (having a child in the nursery drop a toy on their head). Dangers permeate life from the first breath outside the womb to the last breath before the grave.

When our babies were called straight into the arms of Jesus, to a place where "the wicked cease from troubling" and where "the weary are at rest" (Job 3:17), they were spared from all these dangers. We experience the current anguish of living without them, but they are experiencing the joy of safety with Christ. After the death of his three children, Thomas Smyth said:

> How merciful, and how kind is it, therefore, in early years, for the good Shepherd to snatch His young lambs from the jaws of the wolf, the temptations of a wicked world, and a growingly wicked heart; from the cold blasts of wintry adversity, to those blissful regions, where the sun shall no more go down, nor the moon withdraw herself; where He, who is on the throne, shall be their everlasting light, and their days of mourning shall be ended.[1]

We know that the longer we live in this world, the more hardships we will experience. Yes, in God's kindness there are countless joys as well, but the pilgrimage to our heavenly home is marked by suffering. Jesus warns us: "In this world you will have trouble" (John 16:33 NIV). Our babies have been spared the "many tribulations" a Christian must go through to enter the kingdom of God (Acts 14:22). They have "gained the crown without the turmoil."[2] Of course, given the choice, we would take our babies back today. But just think where we would be calling them away from. They are in the arms of Jesus—who alone can provide complete and permanent safety.

A SURE HOPE

When we lowered Leila's body into the grave, I put the first handful of soil on top of her coffin. "See you soon," I whispered through tears. After Leila died, there were some friends and family who expressed gladness that I had my faith to get me through this. They were relieved that Jonny and I had the comfort of believing that we would see Leila again, even if they didn't believe it themselves. So how can I be sure that I will, in fact, see my daughter again? On what basis can we believe that our babies really are "safe in the arms of Jesus"? I have come to see that there are two main reasons: God's covenant and Christ's invitation.

God's covenant

In Psalm 22, King David declares that "from my mother's womb you have been my God" (v. 10). David knew that God's covenant faithfulness ran from parents to children. He believed God's words in Genesis 17:7: "And I will establish my covenant between me and you and your offspring after you throughout their generations for an everlasting covenant, to be God to you and to your offspring after you." What if David had died in his mother's womb? Could his mother have confidence that he had gone to heaven? Absolutely. Even while David was an unborn baby, God was his God.

David faces the same question of assurance years later when his own baby son is taken from him in death. He says with confidence, "But now he is dead. Why should I fast? Can I bring him back again? *I shall go to him, but he will not return to me*" (2 Samuel 12:23). David is not speaking here of the grave, but as John Calvin says, of "the hope that he had of life after death."[3] If David was sure that one day he would be reunited with his son after death, can we not have the same assurance? For his God is our God, and he cannot be untrue to his covenant promises to us and to our children.

Christ's invitation

The second reason I am persuaded that I will see Leila again in heaven, is Christ's invitation to children. In the Gospels we see Jesus's love for infants as he beckons them to come to him:

> Then children were brought to him that he might lay his hands on them and pray. The disciples rebuked the people, but Jesus said, "Let the little children come to me and do not hinder them, *for to such belongs the kingdom of heaven.*" And he laid his hands on them and went away. (Matthew 19:13–15)

Calvin says that Jesus's response to children here shows us that "God adopts infants and washes them in the blood of his Son . . . they are regarded by Christ as among his flock."[4] The disciples viewed the children as a nuisance and a disruption to "real" ministry, but Jesus opens his arms and welcomes them. As the Good Shepherd, he gathers children like little lambs into his flock.

Of course, our babies gain access to heaven only through Jesus, whom they need as much as any other sinner. They too must be washed, sanctified, and justified by the blood of Christ. Calvin again, writing on this passage in Matthew 19, says, "[I]f they must be left among the children of Adam, they are left in death, for in Adam we can only die. On the contrary, Christ commands them to be brought to Him. Why? Because He is life. To give them life therefore He makes them partakers of Himself."[5]

After Leila was stillborn, we had a full autopsy done to see if we could discern the cause of her death.

Nothing conclusive was found. If we are asked why Leila died, our answer is simply that Jesus called her name, and she went to him. The same is true of your child, however they died. Jesus called their name, and they went to him. He welcomed them into his arms. He welcomed them into his kingdom.

Much has been written on this subject, but I am convinced, as many before me have been and continue to be, that our babies are safe in heaven by virtue of God's covenant and Christ's invitation. In this conviction, I stand in the company of John Calvin, William Tyndale, Samuel Rutherford, Cotton Mather, Matthew Henry, John Owen, George Whitefield, Isaac Watts, Augustus Toplady, Thomas Smyth, B. B. Warfield, and many others who have studied this question in much greater depth than me.

One of the clearest statements on the confidence parents can have when their covenant children die in the womb or in infancy was made by the delegates at the Synod of Dort in 1618–1619. They penned the Canons of Dort, articles that have become popularly known as "The Five Points of Calvinism." Here's what they wrote:

> Since we are to judge the will of God from his Word, which testifies that the children of believers are holy, not by nature, but in virtue of the covenant of grace, in which they together with their parents are comprehended, godly parents ought not to doubt the election and salvation of their children whom it pleases God to call out of this life in their infancy. (1.17)

In the light of this tradition of godly Christian ministers who have held this conviction, "we ought not to doubt" but instead have the sure hope that we will see our babies in heaven one day.

A CERTAIN REUNION

Scripture pictures heaven as a place where the multitude of God's elect are gathered, from nursing infants and weaned children (Isaiah 11:8), to saints who lived to an old age on earth. The celestial city will be full of boys and girls playing in its streets (Zechariah 8:4–5). Our babies have gone before us to the heavenly courts, and they are waiting there for us. As Thomas Smyth says:

> Can we not with David rejoicingly declare, "They cannot come to us, but we can go to them?" Yes, we can go to them. They are not lost, but gone before. There in that world of light, and love, and joy, they await our coming. There do they beckon us to ascend. There do they stand ready to welcome us.[6]

My daughter Leila is there, and so too is your baby. They are ready to welcome us home. And in the meantime, we have a wonderful assurance:

> *Safe in the arms of Jesus,*
> *safe from corroding care,*
> *safe from the world's temptations,*
> *sin cannot harm them there.*
>
> Fanny J. Crosby[7]

9

The Pain Will Change

Come and let us return unto the Lord;
for He hath torn and He will heal us;
He hath smitten and He will bind us up.

Thomas Smyth

NEVER THE SAME AGAIN

In the days between finding out that Leila had died and waiting for her birth, I remember feeling like I had become a completely different person overnight. In one instant my life changed, and I wondered if "the old Jackie" was gone forever. An email from a mother whose twins were stillborn years earlier confirmed what I feared was true:

> You will never be the same, Jackie. That is the truth of it. Grief has taken up her place in your heart and she is now a part of you. The loss of a child is a piercing and indescribable pain, and it changes you forever.

At the time, I didn't like facing this reality. I wanted life before Leila's death back—life when cares were few and joys were many. Would I ever laugh again? Would I ever again be able to enjoy simple pleasures, like a really good flat white, or an evening out with friends? Right after Leila's death it seemed like everything good in the world had lost its sweetness. I felt self-conscious seeing friends again, wondering how different I must now seem to them. I wanted to cling to the person I was before death darkened my door.

It's now seven years later, and I have experienced the truth of the words in that email. I am not the same person I was before Leila died. The trauma of my devastating loss has etched itself onto my heart and body. Grief has taken up residence in my heart and is now my companion for life. Sometimes its presence is loud and clanging, and other times it is tucked away and so quiet that I forget for a moment that it is there. But grief is there. And whenever I feel that pang in my heart, I remember that Leila's death has changed me.

DEEP WOUNDS

When death snatches a baby from your womb or your arms, the wounds left behind are deep. They won't look the same for each of us, but suffering always leaves a mark. For me, one of the most serious impacts of stillbirth has been the effect of the trauma on my brain and body. After Leila's death, I became convinced that I was going to be the next to die. In the weeks, months, and years following her death, I experienced obsessive, anxious thoughts related to my health. Any mild pain, dizziness, breathlessness, or other physical symptoms led me to believe it was a sign of an undiagnosed terminal illness. I became obsessed with googling my symptoms on my phone, often scrolling endlessly in the middle of the night, while Jonny lay asleep beside me. I went from medical appointment to medical appointment, expecting the pronouncement of a malignant diagnosis that never came. I was holding my breath waiting for the next terrible thing to happen.

I also felt high levels of anxiety about the health and safety of my living children. After three years of trying to conceive following Leila's death, the Lord opened my womb and graciously gave us another daughter. It isn't an exaggeration to say that I spent a lot of the pregnancy fearing, and expecting, that she would die. Following a stillbirth, I had a lot of extra monitoring during the pregnancy. If ever my daughter's heart rate slowed down during one of the checkups, panic would flood my body. I would automatically assume this was the moment when her heart would slow to a stop. Jonny and I have also had multiple mornings where we wake up to the sound of two children awake and chattering, but the third, completely quiet. When this happens, we both look at each other knowingly, fearing the worst, before one of us quickly goes to check that they are still breathing. In the months, even years, following Leila's death, it felt like I was in a perpetual brace position, waiting for the plane to crash.

I wish some of the debriefing in the hospital after stillbirth had included information about post-traumatic stress disorder (PTSD). No medical professional talked to me about the way trauma and stress can impact the body and lead to actual changes in brain structure and pathways. Every time I sensed danger (real or perceived), my sensitive fight-or-flight response would send my body into hyperarousal, cortisol flooding my body. It got to the point where I was almost in a constant state of panic. Doctors explain that PTSD can be characterized by intrusive thoughts, hyperarousal, flashbacks, nightmares and sleep disturbances, changes in memory and concentration, and startle responses.[1] This is not an uncommon experience for women who have suffered the trauma of a stillbirth or miscarriage. My loss didn't just affect me emotionally, but physically and mentally too. It marked my earthly body irreversibly. This is one of the complex ways grief left its mark.

HE BINDS THEM UP

But thankfully, God did not abandon me in my suffering. He drew near. He not only cared about my wounds, he came close to treat them. I have experienced what the psalmist says:

> He heals the brokenhearted
> and binds up their wounds. (Psalm 147:3)

This is the God who meets us in our sorrow and suffering—God the healer, God the physician. That healing will not be complete until the new creation, but the process has begun.

Despite the irreversible impact of suffering in my life, I have experienced many balms that have come from the healing hand of the Lord over the past seven years: the weekly balm of meeting with God's people and hearing his Word taught at church; devotional times in Scripture, praying, journaling; reading books about suffering written by godly saints who have walked similar paths before me;[2] Christian counseling that helped me process my loss and understand its impact; time with family and friends who were willing to listen and walk the dark path with me; even doctor's appointments that helped me to see that my physical symptoms didn't actually point to something more serious.

Because of God's healing, my wounds aren't as raw and painful as they were right after Leila's death. While I am still prone to anxious and catastrophizing thoughts, God is weakening their grip on my heart, helping me to step outside of them and prayerfully view them more rationally. The waves of grief that felt relentless early on have abated, and the tears don't flow as often. That doesn't mean I am not hit by an unexpected wave every now and again, but the pain has softened, and its edges aren't as sharp. And that's because God is at work in me, binding up my wounds and healing my broken heart.

JOY COMES IN THE MORNING

The darkness that floods your world right after the death of your baby is vast. Our tear-filled eyes cannot see beyond it. In those early days of grief, I asked a friend whose son was stillborn years earlier if I was going to survive this. She assured me that, by God's grace, I would. As time passed, glimmers of light started to break through the darkness.

> Weeping may tarry for the night,
>> but joy comes with the morning. (Psalm 30:5)

Weeping doesn't last forever. Right after Leila's death, I doubted that I would ever laugh again. But I did come to laugh again. It took time—many months, in fact. But the laughter did return. In the past seven years

I have enjoyed countless moments of laughter, and have savored many an excellent flat white and plenty of joyous meals with friends. Of course, my healing is not complete. Grief is still a part of me, a quiet companion who accompanies me wherever I go. That's because the final morning hasn't yet come, the morning when Jesus will return and make all things new; the morning when our wounds will be fully healed; the bright and glorious morning when "He will wipe away every tear from their eyes, and death shall be no more, neither shall there be mourning, nor crying, nor pain anymore, for the former things have passed away" (Revelation 21:4). True and everlasting joy will not come tomorrow morning, but it will come on *that* morning. And so we pray, "Come, Lord Jesus!" (Revelation 22:20).

> *Be still, my soul; when dearest friends depart*
> *and all is darkened in the vale of tears,*
> *then you will better know his love, his heart,*
> *who comes to soothe your sorrows and your fears.*
> *Be still, my soul; your Jesus can repay*
> *from his own fullness all he takes away.*
>
> *Be still, my soul; the hour is hast'ning on*
> *when we shall be forever with the Lord,*
> *when disappointment, grief, and fear are gone,*
> *sorrow forgot, love's purest joys restored.*
> *Be still my soul; when change and tears are past,*
> *all safe and blessed we shall meet at last.*

Katharina von Schlegel

10

All Things for Good?

God's people are never so exalted as when they are brought low, never so enriched as when they are emptied, never so advanced as when they are set back by adversity, never so near the crown as when under the cross.

Theodore Cuyler

A COMFORTING VERSE?

Soon after Leila died a few well-meaning people thought it might be helpful to remind me of Romans 8:28: "And we know that for those who love God all things work together for good, for those who are called according to his purpose." I remember recoiling from the reminder. My daughter was barely in the grave, my body was still broken from labor and pregnancy, and I would never see Leila again this side of heaven. How could the death of my daughter work together for my good? I just wanted my baby back.

Despite their good intentions, right after a terrible loss is not usually the best time to share this Bible verse.[1] When you are reeling from the fresh pain of a stillbirth or miscarriage, you can hardly lift your head above the water to catch your breath, let alone climb a mountain to get a bird's-eye perspective on your suffering. When you are in such pain, it is almost impossible to see beyond it or to think about what God is doing through it. But as distance has grown between Leila's death and the present day, I have begun to see some of the ways that Romans 8:28 *is* true, even in the death of my daughter.

CONFORMED TO CHRIST

The verse following Romans 8:28 unpacks one of the ways God works all things together for our good: "For those whom he foreknew he also predestined to be conformed to the image of his Son, in order that he might be the firstborn among many brothers" (Romans 8:29). During our pilgrimage on this earth, from our conception to our grave, God is in the business of transforming us more and more into the image of Christ. He is a man of sorrows, acquainted with grief, a man who was pierced and crushed and wounded (Isaiah 53:5). Becoming more like him, therefore, is a painful process. Tim Challies writes: "[I]f it was only through suffering that Christ himself was made perfect as our Savior, it should be no surprise that it is only through suffering that I am made perfect as his imitator."[2]

One of the pictures Jesus uses to describe himself is the Good Shepherd. In John 10:3–4 he says:

The sheep hear his voice, and he calls his own
sheep by name and leads them out. When he
has brought out all his own, he goes before
them, and the sheep follow him, for they know
his voice.

When you follow someone, it means you are walking a path that they have already walked. When I was
younger, my dad would take our family on lots of hikes.
He would lead the way along the path, not always staying to the marked routes, but taking us to more scenic,
hidden places off the beaten path. Knowing that my dad
was walking ahead of me gave me confidence that the
path was safe. It wasn't always easy—in fact, it was often
a lot of hard work—but I trusted that my dad knew the
way and so I followed him. How much more can we
have the confidence to follow our Good Shepherd? The
places we tread have first been marked by the feet of
our Lord. When he leads us through the valley of the
shadow of death, we know that he is right there ahead
of us, carrying his cross.

In her poem "No Scar?" Amy Carmichael, an Irish
missionary to India, writes about the anomaly of a Christian life lived with no scars, a life that has no resemblance
to the suffering Savior. The final stanza reads:

No wound? No scar?
Yet, as the Master shall the servant be,
And piercèd are the feet that follow Me.
But thine are whole; can he have followed far
Who hast no wound or scar?[3]

If as believers we are truly united to Christ, is it possible to get to the end of our lives bearing no family resemblance to our Older Brother? How can we receive the benefits of being united to Jesus without also carrying the cross of Jesus? Romans 8:16–17 says, "The Spirit himself bears witness with our spirit that we are children of God, and if children, then heirs—heirs of God and fellow heirs with Christ, *provided we suffer with him* in order that we may also be glorified with him." As I walked through the suffering of my daughter's death, receiving scars along the way, God was conforming me more and more to the image of his Son.

A COMFORT TO OTHERS

In the wake of Leila's death, I wanted to talk to women who had scars like Jesus. I wanted to spend time with women who had walked through the valley of the shadow of death, following their Shepherd. I wanted to be with women who had experienced stillbirth but who were still clinging to their Savior. One of the most tender provisions from the Lord in my season of sorrow were sisters in Christ who had themselves been through this affliction, and who therefore knew how to comfort me with the comfort they had received. They reminded me of the words of the apostle Paul when he says:

> Blessed be the God and Father of our Lord Jesus Christ, the Father of mercies and God of all comfort, who comforts us in all our affliction, so that we may be able to comfort those who are in any affliction, with the comfort with which we ourselves are comforted by God. (2 Corinthians 1:3–4)

I am sure that God will provide similar companions in grief for you. And one day it will be your turn to comfort others. The Lord will put women across your path who have experienced the pain of miscarriage or stillbirth and will be looking for a sister who understands some of what they're going through. They will search for someone who can look them in the eye and assure them that God will be an ever-present help in *their* time of trouble. They will be looking for someone with scars, someone who looks like Jesus.

Seven years from Leila's death, I look at my life and see a pile of precious gems that I have received through the trials of suffering.[4] Has this made Leila's death worth it? No. Her death is still a result of the curse and is not "good" in itself. Why she died will remain a mystery until heaven. But God has not wasted one bit of my suffering. He is the God who refines through fire, who is conforming me more and more into the image of his Son. While initially I recoiled at the reminder of Romans 8:28, I have begun to see that "the good I have received from my sorrows, and pains, and griefs, is altogether incalculable."[5]

> *It is not thou that shapest God,*
> *it is God that shapest thee.*
> *If thou art the work of God,*
> *await the hand of the artist*
> *who does all things in due season.*
> *Offer Him thy heart,*
> *soft and tractable,*
> *and keep the form*
> *in which the artist has fashioned thee.*

Let thy clay be moist,
lest thou grow hard
and lose the imprint of his fingers.

Irenaeus

11

Heaven Is Our Home

*As soon as our souls pass into glory we will see
Jesus . . . . We will not feel strange or out of place,
but profoundly and permanently home.*

Edward Donnelly

DISPLACED

I have never felt so displaced on the earth as I did
when Leila died. When we would leave our house in
the days just after her death, I felt like I was removed
from reality, watching everything in a kind of trance.
I couldn't believe that for others life was just continuing as normal, that people were going about their daily
business seemingly without a care. I wanted to shout at
them: "Don't you know that my baby just died?! Why
are you acting as if nothing has changed when *everything* has changed?" When a loved one dies, it is shock-
ing to notice that life keeps moving forward. I couldn't

believe that the sun kept rising each morning, gravity continued to keep us grounded, and people kept going to work each day. Everything that once seemed normal about our world suddenly felt foreign. I was seeing the world through a new lens, and I felt completely out of place.

HOMESICK FOR HEAVEN

The apostle Paul reminds us that "our citizenship is in heaven. And we eagerly await a Savior from there, the Lord Jesus Christ" (Philippians 3:20 NIV). I had known this was true for many years, but it wasn't until Leila's death that I *felt* it to be true. When life is pleasant, it is very easy to snuggle into the comforts of this world and feel at home here. We love putting down roots and settling down. But it is not until our foundations here are shaken that we acutely feel that our citizenship is on another shore, that this world is not our home. As Thomas Watson, a Puritan preacher, once said, "When God lays men upon their backs, then they look up to heaven."[1]

There is also something unique about the death of a child that pulls our heartstrings to another world. A part of us has been transplanted and sent ahead, and we long to go to the heavenly country where they now live. When I was younger and was taught that Jesus could return at any moment, I remember asking him to hold off until various events had taken place in my life. From a trip to Disneyland to getting married one day, I prayed that Jesus wouldn't come back until after I had enjoyed some of those experiences. I now laugh at the naiveté of my younger self, but it's not uncommon for adults to think this way too. When Leila died suddenly,

I longed with all my being for Jesus to come back right away, take me to heaven, and make all things new. Suffering makes us homesick for heaven.

The apostle Paul talks about this feeling of homesickness in his Second Letter to the Corinthians. He too felt the precariousness of his earthly home and longed for the permanence of his heavenly home:

> For we know that if the tent that is our earthly home is destroyed, we have a building from God, a house not made with hands, eternal in the heavens. For in this tent we groan, longing to put on our heavenly dwelling, if indeed by putting it on we may not be found naked. For while we are still in this tent, we groan, being burdened—not that we would be unclothed, but that we would be further clothed, so that what is mortal may be swallowed up by life. (2 Corinthians 5:1–4)

Suffering makes us groan for our eternal building in the heavens. God helps us to see this earthly home for what it is: a temporary, movable tent, flapping in the wind, held in place by a few pegs. When our child is sent ahead, this earthly dwelling place no longer has the allure it did before. Theodore Cuyler writes, "Happy is that child of Jesus who is always listening for the footfall this side of the golden gate, and for the voice of the invitation to hurry home. A true life is just a tarrying in the tent for Christ until we go into the mansion with Christ."[2] Listening for the footfall and tarrying in the tent changes our lives this side of eternity. Since Leila's death, it has been when my eyes are downcast and looking only at the world around me that I have felt closest to despair. When I live by sight, I only see what is missing—my Leila, and I can easily become consumed by my loss and grief. But when I live by faith (2 Corinthians 5:7), I see what is coming—my heavenly home.

SOJOURNING ON EARTH

Looking forward to the heavenly city means that we live as sojourners on this earth, like our spiritual forefathers Abraham, Isaac, and Jacob. This life is a temporary pilgrimage, and we are just passing through as we travel to that eternal shore. Being a sojourner means that I must hold all things with an open hand, including my children; Leila's death taught me that. My children don't belong to me, and they are not my possession. Treasures here can be ours one day and gone the next. But in heaven, our treasures are stored in a place "where neither moth nor rust destroys and where thieves do not break in and steal" (Matthew 6:20).

As a sojourner, I have also learned that there is nothing certain in this life. A week before Leila's due date, Jonny and I were like most couples nearing the end of pregnancy. Expectant. Anxious. Excited. We were doing the usual things parents do to prepare: washing outfits, stocking up on diapers, and reading books to Ben about becoming a big brother. There are only happy endings in those books. And there wasn't a shadow of doubt in our minds that we'd have one too, with the birth of our second child. How presumptuous we were.

> Now listen, you who say, "Today or tomorrow we will go to this or that city, spend a year there,

carry on business and make money." Why, you
do not even know what will happen tomorrow.
(James 4:13–14 NIV)

This doesn't mean that it is wrong to buy diapers and
wash baby clothes before the hoped-for birth of a child.
But I have learned firsthand that we cannot just pre-
sume it will happen. During my next pregnancy three
years later, our mindset was so different. We prayed a lot
more for the safety of our baby; we enjoyed milestones
of growth and development, but we knew that at any
moment this baby might be taken from us too. When
we talked about her arrival, we always added, "Lord
willing," and we meant it. I still feel nervous when I see
couples announce a pregnancy on social media and tell
the world that their baby *will* be arriving in a particular
month. "Lord willing," I pray. This is true, not just for
the safe arrival of a child, but regarding all our plans
in this life. Except for God's Word and the hope of the
gospel, nothing is certain until we get to heaven.

HOME

One glorious day our sojourn on this earth will come
to an end. When you're in the midst of sorrow, that day
feels very far away. But as Spurgeon writes, even "in the
darkest of all human sorrows there is the glad prospect
that the day will break, and the shadows will flee away."[3]
On that day, Isaiah tells us:

> The sun shall be no more
>   your light by day,
> nor for brightness shall the moon
>   give you light;

but the LORD will be your everlasting light,
   and your God will be your glory.
Your sun shall no more go down,
   nor your moon withdraw itself;
for the LORD will be your everlasting light,
   and your days of mourning shall be ended.
                  (Isaiah 60:19–20)

It will be a wondrous day when our mourning is over, and we are reunited with our children in heaven. But even more wondrous will be meeting our Savior, the Lord Jesus, who is preparing a place for us in his Father's house. Heaven will only be heaven because he is there. When Jesus was still on earth and his disciples were troubled, he comforted them with this promise: "I will come again and will take you *to myself*, that where *I am* you may be also" (John 14:3). One day we will depart and be *with Christ*, and then we will be *in heaven* forever. Then we will be profoundly and permanently home.

> *O sweet and blessed country,*
> *the home of God's elect!*
> *O sweet and blessed country,*
> *that eager hearts expect!*
> *Jesus, in mercy bring us*
> *to that dear land of rest;*
> *who are, with God the Father,*
> *and Spirit, ever blest.*

                  Bernard of Cluny

12

After Winter, Spring

*Their bodies will come forth out of their graves to
meet them, incorruptible, immortal, powerful,
glorious, and all death-divided Christian friends
shall meet to part no more.*

John Brown

NOT YET BEST

The separation of body and soul was never more real
to me than when I was holding my daughter's lifeless
body in the hospital. Up until that point, I thought
that somehow Leila must already be with Jesus, bodily.
And yet, here was her very real body in my arms—all
seven pounds of it—the same very real body that would
soon lie in a little, white coffin and be buried in a grave
here on earth. Yes, her soul was already with the Lord,
which was "far better" (Philippians 1:23), but was it yet
best? Was this the end of her story? Sitting in that hospital room holding my baby's tiny, precious body, I was
struck that there was more to come.

THE FIRSTFRUITS

We see this same separation of body and soul on Good
Friday. On the cross, Jesus's final words to his Father
were "into your hands I commit my spirit!" (Luke 23:46);
but, as we know after he died, his body was committed
to the grave. His soul and body were separated from
Friday evening until Sunday morning. In the same way,
when our babies died, their souls went immediately to
heaven, but their bodies went to the grave. It would be a
tragic story if that were the end. But it is not the end. On
that Sunday morning, when Jesus rose from the dead,
his soul and body were reunited, never to be separated
again. And the good news is that Jesus is "the firstfruits
of those who have fallen asleep" (1 Corinthians 15:20),
which means your baby's life, death, and resurrection
pattern that of the Lord. When a tree or a vine bears its
first-of-the-season fruit, we all know there is more fruit
coming.

At Leila's graveside committal service, our minister opened with these words: "The enduring hope of the
Christian faith is not the immortality of the soul, but
the resurrection of the body." We rejoiced that Leila's
soul was with the Lord Jesus and that she was perfectly
safe, but we knew that wasn't the end for her. We were
looking ahead to a future hope that was not yet a reality.
Leila was, and still is, awaiting her resurrection body—
her glorious, new-creation, imperishable body. Her
story isn't yet complete. To mark this already-but-not-
yet part of Leila's story, we had three words engraved
on her coffin: "Awaiting the Resurrection." However or
wherever you laid your baby's body to rest, he or she
is awaiting that same resurrection, when "the trumpet
will sound, and the dead will be raised imperishable"

(1 Corinthians 15:52). The best is yet to come, which gives their little bodies huge significance—even in death.

THE BODY

In Philippians, the apostle Paul writes, "We await a Savior, the Lord Jesus Christ, who will transform our lowly body to be like his glorious body" (Philippians 3:20b–21a). This means that our babies' bodies, lowly though they were, *matter*. They have eternal significance because it is their very bodies that will be transformed into resurrection glory.

Jonny and I felt the importance of Leila's body when we spent two days in the hospital with her after she was stillborn. Some people might think it strange that we spent so much time with our deceased daughter; maybe it feels macabre to some. But parents who have experienced the death of their baby can probably relate. I have spoken with many mothers who did special things with and for their babies even after their death; bathing them, clothing them, getting imprints of their hands and feet, cutting a lock of hair, taking photos, cuddling them, kissing them, holding their tiny hands, reading them books, singing them songs. I have spoken to mothers who have experienced the pain of miscarriage who looked carefully for any signs of their baby's body during the loss, desperate to see some physical form of their beloved offspring. In the past, stillborn babies were whisked away immediately after birth, and parents weren't given the chance to touch or hold their babies. Thankfully, things have changed a great deal, and many hospitals now have much better ways of honoring stillborn babies and their parents. Every mother feels the importance of her child's body, which is why leaving them behind is so agonizing.

The significance of our earthly bodies can be seen in how Jesus's body was cared for after he died. Joseph of Arimathea took his body, wrapped it in clean linen and laid it in a new tomb (Matthew 27:59–60). Some women who had come with Jesus from Galilee brought spices and ointments to anoint his body (Luke 23:55–56), and Nicodemus brought about seventy-five pounds worth of myrrh and aloes for the same purpose (John 19:39). Why was Jesus's body so precious and treated as such? Because his body was part of his person. The Gospel writers speak often with reference to Jesus's body as "him" not "it." John is most explicit: after stating that Joseph of Arimathea took Jesus's body and wrapped it in linen, he writes that they laid *Jesus* in the tomb (John 19:42). Our personhood is not simply our soul; it is comprised of our soul *and* body. And because Jesus the *person* was raised from the dead, so too was his body. We stayed for two days in the hospital with *Leila*. We said a tearful goodbye to *her*.

THE END AND THE BEGINNING

In 1 Corinthians 15, Paul describes our earthly bodies as seeds that are sown to produce something much greater when Christ returns. God won't start from scratch on that day; instead, he will use that kernel and turn it into something glorious:

> So is it with the resurrection of the dead. What is sown is perishable; what is raised is imperishable. It is sown in dishonor; it is raised in glory. It is sown in weakness; it is raised in power. It

is sown a natural body; it is raised a spiritual
body. If there is a natural body, there is also a
spiritual body. (1 Corinthians 15:42–44)

Our babies are like little seeds planted in the ground
awaiting the Gardener's call to spring forth from the
flower bed of his sacred acre.[1]

At the end of *The Last Battle*, C. S. Lewis's final
installment of the Narnia series, Lucy learns that they
have entered "heaven" at last. They have begun new-
creation life, so to speak.

> And for us this is the end of all the stories, and
> we can most truly say that they all lived hap-
> pily ever after. But for them it was only the
> beginning of the real story. All their life in this
> world and all their adventures had only been
> the cover and the title page: now at last they
> were beginning Chapter One of the Great Story
> which no one on earth has read: which goes on
> forever: in which every chapter is better than
> the one before.[2]

And so it is for our children who died in infancy.
They are listening for the final trumpet. They are waiting for the day when they will rise from the earth so
that they can begin Chapter One of the Great Story that
goes on forever, in which every chapter is better than
the one before. Happily ever after, indeed!

THE DAFFODILS

A week before Leila died, Ben picked a daffodil from
our backyard and gave it to me. I put it in a little glass

bottle and set it on the mantelpiece. After Leila's death, I remember staring at that single daffodil in amazement, and then looking outside and seeing lots of them standing proudly, waving in the soft, spring breeze. In that moment, daffodils became indelibly connected to our daughter. Wherever we have lived since, we always plant daffodil bulbs in the garden during the fall and then wait for the day their green shoots break through the soil. They remind us every year that winter can never hold back the spring. It is the way God has made his world to work. After darkness, light. After evening, morning. After winter, spring!

Leila was laid to rest in a small English church cemetery. Every spring, the graveyard bursts forth with life: white snowdrops appear first, growing in intimate clusters, bobbing their brave little heads in the frost of early spring; a wildflower garden stretches toward the sun, beckoning butterflies and bees that weave in and out of headstones; rabbits start to emerge from their burrows, nibbling freshly grown grass and bright tulip petals. And then there are the daffodils. So many daffodils, their bright yellow trumpets declaring victory over winter. Color and brilliance burgeon from the same soil that covers the sacred remains of men, women, and children. And one of them is our dark-haired baby girl. She is waiting for the Last Spring to begin. On that day, in the light of the risen sun, the Gardener will appear. And he will say, "Leila, come forth." He will call your baby's name too. And they will all go to him, just as they went when he called them the first time: "Come to me, for to such as you belongs the kingdom of heaven." And as they step out of their resting place onto holy ground, I'm sure the daffodils will be blooming.

See, what a morning, gloriously bright,
With the dawning of hope in Jerusalem;
Folded the grave-clothes, tomb filled with light,
As the angels announce, "Christ is risen!" . . .
And we are raised with Him;
Death is dead, love has won, Christ has conquered.
And we shall reign with Him,
For He lives, Christ is risen from the dead!

Stuart Townend and Keith Getty[3]

Last Words

A Prayer to Join Our Children

Bring us, O Lord God, at our last awakening into the house and gate of heaven, to enter into that gate and dwell in that house, where there shall be no darkness nor dazzling, but one equal light; no noise nor silence, but one equal music; no fears nor hopes, but one equal possession; no ends nor beginnings, but one equal eternity; in the habitation of your glory and dominion, world without end. Amen.[1]

John Donne

Suggestions for Further Reading

Bruce III, James W. *From Grief to Glory: A Book of Comfort for Grieving Parents.* Edinburgh: Banner of Truth, 2008.

Gibson, Jonathan. *The Moon Is Always Round.* Greensboro, NC: New Growth Press, 2019.

Guthrie, Nancy, ed. *Be Still, My Soul: Embracing God's Purpose and Provision in Suffering.* Wheaton, IL: Crossway, 2010.

Guthrie, Nancy. *Holding onto Hope: A Pathway through Suffering to the Heart of God.* Carol Stream, IL: Tyndale Momentum, 2015.

Guthrie, Nancy. *The One-Year Book of Hope: A 365-Day Devotional with Daily Scripture Readings and Uplifting Reflections that Encourage, Comfort, and Restore Joy.* Carol Stream, IL: Tyndale Momentum, 2005.

Ivey, Jonny and Joanna. *Silent Cries: Experiencing God's Love after Losing a Baby.* Nottingham: IVP, 2021.

Lewis, C. S. *A Grief Observed.* San Francisco, CA: HarperOne, 2015.

Smith, Esther. *A Still and Quiet Mind: Twelve Strategies for Changing Unwanted Thoughts.* Phillipsburg, NJ: P&R Publishing, 2022.

Vroegop, Mark. *Dark Clouds, Deep Mercy: Discovering the Grace of Lament.* Wheaton, IL: Crossway, 2019.

Wedgeworth, Abbey. *Held: 31 Biblical Reflections on God's Comfort and Care in the Sorrow of Miscarriage.* Epsom, Surrey: The Good Book Company, 2020.

Endnotes

Preface

1. C. S. Lewis, *The Four Loves* (Hammersmith, London: Harper Collins Publishers, 2002), 78–79.

Chapter 2

1. Thomas Smyth, "The Bereaved Mother," in *Solace for Bereaved Parents* (Columbia, SC: The R. L. Bryan Company, 1912), 172.

2. Theodore Cuyler, *God's Light on Dark Clouds* (Shawnee, KS: Gideon House Books, 2015), 42.

3. Lilias Trotter, *A Blossom in the Desert: Reflections of Faith in the Art and Writings of Lilias Trotter* (Grand Rapids, MI: Our Daily Bread Publishing, 2016), journal entry August 10, 1901.

Chapter 3

1. Anonymous, cited by Dr. John Wyatt in conversation.

2. John Calvin, *The Gospel According to St John 11–21 and the First Epistle of John*, Calvin's New Testament Commentaries, eds. David W. Torrance and Thomas F. Torrance, trans. T. H. L. Parker (Grand Rapids, MI: Eerdmans, 1994), 11.

3. John Eadie, *Words of Comfort for Bereaved Parents*, ed. William Logan (London: The Religious Tract Society, 1874), 127.

4. Edward Payson, *The Complete Works of Edward Payson*, D. D. (Portland, ME: Hyde and Lord, 1849), 93.

Chapter 4

1. Thomas Boston, *The Crook in the Lot* (Edinburgh: Banner of Truth, 2017), 3.
2. Boston, *The Crook in the Lot*, 3 (emphasis added by author).
3. Boston, *The Crook in the Lot*, 17.
4. Westminster Confession of Faith, 3.1.

Chapter 5

1. Abraham Kuyper, *To Be Near unto God* (Grand Rapids, MI: Christian Classics Ethereal Library, 1918), 106.
2. These ideas are derived from Jonathan Gibson, *The Moon Is Always Round* (Greensboro, NC: New Growth Press, 2019).
3. Christopher Ash, *Job: The Wisdom of the Cross* (Wheaton, IL: Crossway, 2014), 374.
4. John J. Murray, *Behind a Frowning Providence* (Edinburgh: Banner of Truth, 1990), 22.

Chapter 6

1. These development milestones come from Mark Jones, *If I Could Speak: Letters from the Womb* (Ross-shire: Christian Focus, 2020).
2. Francis Crick, quoted in *Pacific News Service*, January 1978.
3. Emphasis added by author; and hereafter when italics are used in a passage of Scripture.
4. R. C. Sproul, *Abortion: A Rational Look at an Emotional Issue* (Colorado Springs, CO: NavPress, 1990), 53–54.

Chapter 7

1. Nora Seton, *The Kitchen Congregation: Gatherings at the Hearth* (London: Picador, 2000), 26.

Chapter 8

1. Anonymous, "Views of a Troubled Father. In a Letter to the Author," in Thomas Smyth, *Solace for Bereaved Parents* (Columbia, SC: The R. L. Bryan Company, 1912), 158.

2. Smyth, *Solace for Bereaved Parents*, 197.

3. John Calvin, *Sermons on 2 Samuel: Chapters 1–13*, trans. Douglas J. Kelly (Edinburgh: Banner of Truth, 1992), 592.

4. John Calvin, *Institutes of the Christian Religion* (Philadelphia, PA: The Westminster Press, 1970): book 4, chapter 16, section 31, volume 2, 460 (cf. also 461, 456, 436, 435).

5. John Calvin, cited in Smyth, *Solace for Bereaved Parents*, 24.

6. Smyth, *Solace for Bereaved Parents*, 213.

7. Fanny J. Crosby had only one child who died soon after birth.

Chapter 9

1. J. Douglas Bremner, "Traumatic Stress: Effects on the Brain," from The National Library of Medicine, https://www.ncbi.nlm.nih.gov/pmc/articles/PMC3181836/.

2. See "Suggestions for Further Reading" at the end of this book.

Chapter 10

1. If you are reading this book as someone who would like to better understand and support a friend who has experienced loss, I recommend Nancy Guthrie's book, *What Grieving People Wish You Knew about What Really Helps (and What Really Hurts)* (Wheaton, IL: Crossway, 2016).

2. Tim Challies, *Seasons of Sorrow: The Pain of Loss and the Comfort of God* (Grand Rapids, MI: Zondervan Reflective, 2022), bonus chapters, 10.

3. Amy Carmichael, *Toward Jerusalem* (Fort Washington, PA: CLC Publications, 2003), 95.

4. F. B. Meyer, *The Secret of Guidance* (Chicago, IL: Fleming H. Revell Company, 1896), 95: "Sorrow is a mine,

the walls of which glisten with precious stones; be sure and do not retrace your steps into daylight without some specimens."

5. C. H. Spurgeon, cited in Darrel W. Amundsen, "The Anguish and Agonies of Charles Spurgeon," *Christian History* 29:1 (1991): 25.

Chapter 11

1. John J. Murray, *Behind a Frowning Providence* (Edinburgh: Banner of Truth, 1990), 19.

2. Theodore Cuyler, *God's Light on Dark Clouds* (Shawnee, KS: Gideon House Books, 2015), 84.

3. C. H. Spurgeon, "Darkness before the Dawn," in *The Metropolitan Tabernacle Pulpit Sermons* (London: Passmore & Alabaster, 1896), 375.

Chapter 12

1. The expression "sacred acre" alludes to Henry Wadsworth Longfellow's poem "God's Acre," in *The Complete Poetical Works of Henry Wadsworth Longfellow* (Boston and New York: Houghton, Mifflin and Company, 1894), 37.

2. C. S. Lewis, *The Last Battle* (Glasgow: Collins, 2001), 224.

3. Stuart Townend and Keith Getty, "See What a Morning," https://store.gettymusic.com/us/song/see-what-a-morning/. Reprinted with permission.

Last Words

1. The prayer by John Donne (1572–1631) is adapted from a sermon he preached at Whitehall on Acts 7:60, February 29, 1627. See *Daily Prayer*, eds. Eric Milner-White and G. W. Briggs (Harmondsworth, UK: Penguin, 1959), http://assets.newscriptorium.com/collects-and-prayers/daily_prayer.htm.